Rough

25 Ultimate experiences

China

Make the most of your time on Earth

ROUGH
GUIDES

25 YEARS 1982–2007

NEW YORK • LONDON • DELHI

Contents

Introduction

EXPERIENCES have always been at the heart of the Rough Guide concept. A group of us began writing the books **25 years ago** (hence this celebratory mini series) and wanted to share the kind of travels we had been doing ourselves. It seems bizarre to recall that in the early 1980s, travel was very much a minority pursuit. Sure, there was a lot of tourism around, and that was reflected in the guidebooks in print, which traipsed around the established sights with scarcely a backward look at the local population and their life. We wanted to change all that: to put a country or a city's popular culture centre stage, to highlight the clubs where you could hear local music, drink with people you hadn't come on holiday with, watch the local football, join in with the festivals. And of course we wanted to push travel a bit further, inspire readers with the confidence and knowledge to break away from established routes, to find pleasure and excitement in remote islands, or desert routes, or mountain treks, or in street culture.

Twenty-five years on, that thinking seems pretty obvious: we all want to experience something real about a destination, and to seek out travel's **ultimate experiences**. Which is exactly where these **25 books** come in. They are not in any sense a new series of guidebooks. We're happy with the series that we already have in print. Instead, the **25s** are a collection of ideas, enthusiasms and inspirations: a selection of the very best things to see or do – and not just before you die, but now. Each selection is gold dust. That's the brief to our writers: there is no room here for the average, no space fillers. Pick any one of our selections and you will enrich your travelling life.

But first of all, take the time to browse. Grab a half dozen of these books and let the ideas percolate … and then begin making your plans.

Mark Ellingham
Founder & Series Editor, Rough Guides

Ultimate
experiences
China

Getting lost *in the* Forbidden City

01

At Beijing's heart is **Gugong**, literally the "Imperial Palace" but more evocatively known as the **Forbidden City**. For hundreds of years this was China's psychic centre despite being barred to all but the **emperor** and his colossal **retinue** of advisors, wives, and eunuchs. Even today, almost a century after the last emperor was deposed, there's nowhere else in China that leaves such a lasting impression of just how **wealthy** the emperors were compared with their subjects, nor how **lonely** and **isolated** they must have been here, their lives regulated to an extraordinary degree by official and religious ceremony. The Forbidden City's boundaries are marked by a tall **red wall** with guard-towers at the corners; red is a lucky colour in China, but the overall effect is austere and, well, forbidding. But nothing prepares you for the awe-inspiring, bleak splendour of the first courtyard, a vast, alienating space paved in grey slabs within which the entire imperial court – **one hundred thousand people** – could assemble at once. Marble bridges cross a ceremonial "stream" here to a succession of red-pillared halls, each housing increasingly grandiose **thrones** where the emperor would fulfil ceremonial functions (**Hall of Supreme Harmony**), receive visitors (**Hall of Protective Harmony**) or spend his wedding nights (**Palace of Earthly Peace**). At the end are the **Imperial Gardens** with their gnarled trees, golden lions and pavilions, but even here the beauty is artificial and structured, and there's no relief from the notion of splendid order and routine – in the middle is the wooded **Hill of Accumulated Elegance**, which the emperor and consort were required to climb every ninth day of the ninth lunar month to admire the scenery.

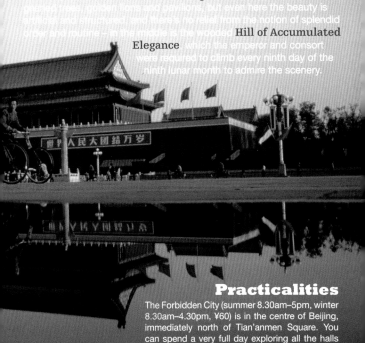

Practicalities

The Forbidden City (summer 8.30am–5pm, winter 8.30am–4.30pm, ¥60) is in the centre of Beijing, immediately north of Tian'anmen Square. You can spend a very full day exploring all the halls and grounds; many people make several visits.

02 Circuiting the Jokhang, Lhasa

The Jokhang is the holiest temple in Tibetan Buddhism, and what it lacks in appearance – a very shabby facade compared with the nearby Potala Palace – it makes up in atmosphere. Sited in the cobbled lanes of the Barkhor district, Lhasa's sole surviving traditional quarter, there's an excited air of reverence as you approach, with a continuous throng of Tibetan pilgrims circuiting the complex anti-clockwise, spinning hand-held prayer wheels and sticking out their tongues at each other in greeting. A good many prostrate themselves at every step, their knees and hands protected from the accumulated battering by wooden pads, which set up irregular clacking noises. Most of the pilgrims are wild-haired Tibetan peasants reeking of yak butter and dressed in

Most of the pilgrims are wild-haired Tibetan peasants reeking of yak butter and dressed in thick, shabby layers

thick, shabby layers against the cold; especially tough-looking are the Khampas from eastern Tibet, who almost always have one arm exposed to the shoulder, whatever the weather.

Devout they may be, but there's absolutely nothing precious about their actions, no air of hushed, respectful reverence – stand still for a second and you'll be knocked aside in the rush to get around. Inside, the various halls are lit by butter lamps, leaving much of the wooden halls rather gloomy and adding a spooky edge to the close-packed saintly statues clothed in multicoloured flags, brocade banners hanging from the ceiling, and especially gory murals of demons draped in skulls and peeling skin off sinners – a far less forgiving picture of Buddhism than the version practised elsewhere in China. The bustle is even more overwhelming here, the crowds increased by red-robed monks, busy topping up the lamps or tidying altars. Make sure you catch the Chapel of Jowo Sakyamuni at the rear of the complex, which sports a beautiful statue of the twelve-year-old Buddha; and the Jokhang's flat roof, where you can look out over the rest of the city.

Practicalities The Jokhang opens daily 8am–6pm (¥70).
As with all Tibetan temples, circuit both the complex and individual halls anti-clockwise.

03

Losing your shirt in Macau

There are few impediments to entry into Macau's best and brightest form of entertainment: if you're over eighteen, are not wearing sandals, shorts or slippers, and you're carrying a passport and are happy to check bags and cameras in at reception, then the management of any one of the territory's seventeen-odd casinos will welcome you in to fritter your hard-earned cash away. Actually, even if you don't gamble, it's worth a look, if only to hang out with the

local Macanese and Hong Kongers who come here to play the weekend away, or the gambling-starved hopefuls who flood over from mainland China. The main hotspot is over on the eastern side of town along kilometre-long Avenida da Amizade, where rival establishments rub elbows within sight of the Outer Port. Each casino has its own atmosphere: notable venues include the legendary *Hotel Lisboa*, with four heavily packed floors

decked out in mock 1930s mirrors, light fittings and wood panelling; the uniquely foreign-owned *Sands*, whose gold-plated glass exterior makes it resemble a pile of bullion; the *Floating Casino*, full of gilded dragon carvings and red wallpaper; and the *Jai-Alai*, an old sports stadium full of hard-faced, downmarket Chinese punters. Most of the punters seem to have a fairly reckless attitude towards

games of chance. One reason for this might be because (rumour has it) some are party bigwigs busy squandering public funds, though none has ever actually been caught in a casino here. If you've been rash enough to ignore the tiny notices at the door ("Betting for fun only, not to get rich") and find funds in short supply, there's a score of pawnbrokers within stumbling distance – their signs look like a bat roosting upside down.

Practicalities

Macau is a 4km-long peninsula jutting out from the Chinese mainland about 60km west of Hong Kong. The border with China is open 7am–midnight, and there are hourly ferries around the clock from Hong Kong. Macau's currency is the pataca (MOP$), though Hong Kong dollars are accepted everywhere at the same face value. All casinos are open twenty-four hours.

04 Henan's *Mona Lisa*

The Buddha's expression – of calm, powerful insight – is, like the Mona Lisa's smile, full of unselfconscious spirit

The term "Buddhist cave art" sounds worthy and dull, conjuring an image of a bald, bearded recluse brightening up his lonely mountain retreat with some crude daubings. Actually, that wouldn't be bad, but the reality is even better. Though the medium here is sculpture, Chinese cave art is closer to the illuminated manuscripts of medieval Christian Europe: holy images in a cartoon format which manage to be comic, exciting and – occasionally – even realistic, without losing the importance of an "inner message".

In China, the idea of carving rockfaces with religious scenes seems to have arrived with the Tobas, one of several regional dynasties who shared power between the break-up of the Han empire in 220 AD and the country's reunification four centuries later under the Tang. They injected central Asian, Indian and Greek influences into Chinese art, while the Buddhist fervour of the Tobas and their Tang successors inspired a trail of rock art sites stretching from northwestern Silk Road oases to the central Chinese heartlands in Henan, where the art form reached a peak at Longmen Caves.

There are over a hundred thousand figures chiselled into a honeycomb of grottoes at Longmen, a task that took even the industrious Chinese four hundred years to complete. Most of the figures are life-sized or smaller, but the biggest and best is a seventeen-metre-high Buddhist trinity whose main figure's ears alone (at over two metres long) humble you into insignificance, whilst almost making you laugh at the proportions. But the Buddha's expression – of calm, powerful insight – is, like the Mona Lisa's smile, full of unselfconscious spirit, a trait which later seeped out of Chinese art, leaving only an institutionalized woodenness.

Practicalities

The Longmen Caves (daily 7am– 6.30pm, ¥80) are 13km south of Louyang city, reached from Louyang's train station on bus #81 (¥1). Two hours is plenty of time to see all the carvings.

Hong Kong

If you like to get on top of everything in your travels, then Hong Kong's summit to conquer is the **552-metre-high** Victoria Peak, about the only thing in Hong Kong island that **outstrips** the eighty-eight-storey **IFC2 Tower**. And unlike everything else to do in the downtown area, not only is **the Peak** (as locals call it) not man-made, but you don't need a wad of cash to enjoy it, at least if you **walk** up – though then you'll lose in **sweat** what you save in money.

It is, however, a great walk through a cross-section of the city, taking you from the harbour, underneath the HSBC Tower and along elevated walkways, around the knife-like Bank of China Tower, into Hong Kong Park. Continue uphill and exit the park near the jaguar cage, then follow ever-steeper inclines between high-rise apartments until the pavement turns into a concrete path and winds up into shady rainforest. Here you'll be overtaken by joggers gasping themselves into an early grave, while the path climbs for another forty minutes past some exclusive, isolated houses (Hong Kong's costliest real estate), and then you're there.

If this all sounds a bit much, then the Peak Tram is a more stylish, faster and less exhausting way to ascend the Peak. In use since the 1880s, the Tram sidesteps the legwork but still gives the feel of the Peak's severe gradients in the way you sink back into your wooden seat as the carriage is hauled upwards. Whichever method you use to conquer the Peak, however, you'll find that reaching the summit brings a sense of let-down in a horrible concrete viewing platform, despite which you'd have to be very hardened not to find the views down on Hong Kong's towering architecture and splendid harbour inspiring.

Practicalities

The Peak is on northern Hong Kong island. If walking, take sunscreen, a hat, and plenty of water – and go early in the morning when it's cooler. Otherwise the Peak Tram runs daily 7am–midnight (HK$20 one-way, HK$30 return, seven minutes); get to the lower Tram terminal on Garden Road by bus #15C from outside the Star Ferry terminal.

06 Joining the pilgrims' trail at
Emei Shan

To start with, Emei is a holy Buddhist site associated with Puxian, the incarnation of Truth, and the mountain's slopes are studded with temples dating back in part to Tang times, which offer travellers wonderfully atmospheric accommodation. And the mountain is also overwhelmingly picturesque, the lower two-thirds covered in thick forests whose plants range from tropical species to high-altitude rhododendrons and camellias – most temples sit immersed in greenery, with wild monkeys and birds roaming about at will.

While many mountains in China are far tougher in terms of gradient, few can rival Emei in terms of distance – the shorter of the two trails to the summit is forty kilometres long, meaning a two-day slog to the top. Dropping into temples along the way breaks the journey: Wannian Si packs the biggest punch, with its life-sized enamelled statue of Puxian riding a six-tusked elephant, but Xianfeng Si and Xixiang Chi – though rather weatherbeaten – are more atmospheric. Your fellow pilgrims are also like to be of interest: either groups of blocky businessmen smoking as they puff along behind their tour guides, or youngsters dressed in blatant disregard of the conditions (men in jackets and leather brogues, women wearing high heels). But you occasionally meet wandering monks too, chanting prayers or thumbing rosaries as they walk, or even locals trying to coax teams of exhausted, heavily-laden horses along the steep paths. Sadly, the forests fade out during the last third of the hike, leaving open moorland and tangled undergrowth, and Emei's top temple is vulgarly over-decorated. But there's a soft touch even here in the dense clumps of padlocks clipped onto the protective railings, left by couples to symbolize their love for each other.

Practicalities

Emei Shan is in Sichuan province, 150km south of the capital, Chengdu. Buses run from Chengdu's Xinnanmen bus station through the day to Baoguo township, at the foot of the mountain (2hr 30min; ¥30); you can also catch a train from Chengdu to Emei town (10 daily; 2hr; ¥30) and a minibus from here to Baoguo (20min; ¥5). Entry to the mountain is ¥120. Allow at least three days for a return hike to the summit, staying at monasteries along the way (¥20 per person for a dormitory bed, ¥250 for a double room with heating if available). Food is basic and relatively expensive. Bring warm clothes for the summit area, which is below freezing from October through to April; you may also need to buy metal cleats or straw sandals off local vendors to stop you slipping on icy stone steps at this time.

07 Faces from the past: Xi'an's Terracotta Army

Qin Shihuang, China's first emperor, never did anything by halves. Not content with building the Great Wall, he spent his last years roaming the fringes of his empire, seeking a key to immortality. When (with inevitable irony) he died on his quest, his entourage returned to the capital near modern-day Xi'an and buried his corpse in a subterranean, city-sized mausoleum whose ceiling was studded with precious stones and where lakes and rivers were represented by mercury.

Or so wrote the historian Sima Qian a century after a popular uprising had overthrown Qin Shihuang's grandson and established the Han dynasty in 206 BC. Nobody knows for sure how true the account is – the tomb remains unexcavated – but in 1974 peasants digging a well nearby found Qin Shihuang's guardians in the afterlife: an army of over ten thousand life-sized terracotta troops arranged in battle formation, filling three huge rectangular vaults.

Make no mistake, the Terracotta Army is not like some giant schoolboy's collection of clay soldiers lined up in ranks under a protective modern hangar. The figures are shockingly human, in a way that makes your skin crawl: each and every one is different, from their facial features to their hands, hairstyles, postures and clothing. They are so individual that you can't help feel that these are real people, tragically fossilized by some natural disaster – more so in places where excavations are incomplete, leaving their half-buried busts gripped by the earth. Even their horses, tethered to the remains of wooden chariots, are so faithfully sculpted that the very breed has been established, as well as – yes, by, examining their teeth – their age.

At the end, there's just one burning question: have they found a statue of Qin Shihuang leading them all? A realistic statue over two thousand years old of China's first emperor – now that surely would be immortality.

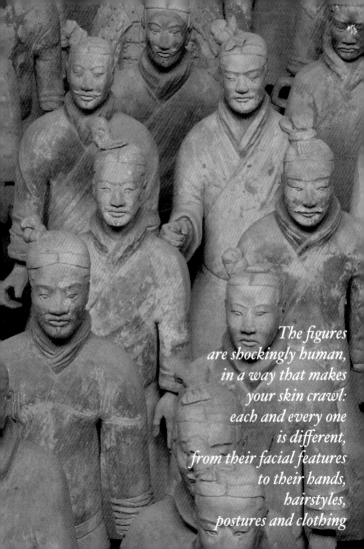

The figures are shockingly human, in a way that makes your skin crawl: each and every one is different, from their facial features to their hands, hairstyles, postures and clothing

Unscrolling
the Li River

You know that **Chinese scroll painting** on the wall of your local takeaway, the one where a river with tiny boats winds between jutting, **strangely shaped peaks**, their tips blurred by clouds? Well, that could be a scene from along the Li River between **Guilin city** and the market town of **Yangshuo** in northern Guangxi province, an eighty-kilometre-long stretch that has provided inspiration to painters and poets for at least the last thousand years.

Today it also **inspires the tourist industry**, but despite the river being almost clogged with **armadas of cruise boats**, the journey still allows a look at the timeless Chinese countryside.

As is often the case in China, however, those expecting a peaceful commune with nature will be disappointed. But get into the **cheerful, noisy Chinese way** of enjoying a day out, and it's great fun: **loaded with food and drink**, head up to the cruise boat's observation deck and watch while the scenery unrolls itself for your pleasure. At first it's all green paddy-fields and **buffaloes wallowing** in the shallows, then the peaks begin to spring up – isolated at first, and none of them much over 200 metres tall, but weathered into fantastic shapes. They all have names too, and legends: this is **Waiting-for-Husband Hill**, where a wife turned to stone waiting for her travelling husband to come home; over there is **Fish-tail Peak** and the Penholder; that rockface is **Nine-horses Fresco Hill**. Tall bamboo screens the bank, source of the rafts which are poled fearlessly over the Li's shoals where cruise boats – flat-bottomed though they are – would founder. **Cormorants** sit on each raft, trained to retrieve fish for their owners; they get to eat every sixth one or refuse to work. And then, around a bend, is **Yangshuo** and the end of the trip; cameras are bagged and jaws are tightened at the sight of **souvenir touts lined up along the pier**.

Practicalities

Li River cruises depart Guilin daily year-round and can be organized through your accommodation or the CITS at 11 Binjiang Lu, ☎0773/2861623, ⓦwww.china4seasons.com for ¥410 per person, including lunch and bus back to Guilin afterwards. The journey takes around six hours, and the best time for cruising is spring through to autumn, when the water level is deep enough to get all the way from Guilin to Yangshuo.

If it's beauty you're after, the small town of Weining in Guizhou province's far western reaches will certainly disappoint. Impoverished, shabby and built up in charmless grey concrete, it is even less appealing than usual if you arrive one frigid night after a shocking six-hour bus ride to find the only hotel's facilities don't include hot water or heating. Or food, for that matter. You'll probably wind up eating grilled potato slices at a roadside barbeque run by women of the Muslim Hui nationality, one of China's many ethnic minority groups. As your mouth buzzes from the amount of chilli they've powdered your dinner with, you'll be relieved to find the journey here hasn't been wasted.

09 *Stalking*
cranes at Caohai

Caohai, the "Grass Sea", is a reed-fringed lake on Weining's outskirts which goes a long way towards making up for the town. A placid spread of water reflecting cloudless skies, it's also the winter residence of four hundred rare black-necked cranes. Seeing these is as easy as renting a punt and poling up to them, an extraordinary liberty in a country where human population pressure makes it unusual (except in markets and on menus) to get on familiar terms with wildlife.

So hire a punt and get out into the maze of channels cut through Caohai's reedy shallows. Weining's traffic, crowds and coal dust will be forgotten in a light breeze, the whisper of the punt pushing through reeds, and small flocks of geese and ducks bobbing on the lake. With luck, you should be able to corner a group or two of cranes, stately creatures stalking through the water, their black heads held high. Considerately, they'll let you get within telephoto range before flapping lazily away to join another distant group. Weining turns out to be not so disappointing after all.

Practicalities

Cranes visit Caohai between November and March. Weining is most easily reached by bus from Anshun, western Guizhou's main town (5hr; ¥36). Accommodation in Weining is either at the *Heijing He hotel* (☎0857/6222048; double with bathroom from ¥150) or any of the numerous basic guesthouses near the bus station (around ¥30 per person). Caohai is a twenty-minute walk south of town, where a punt costs ¥60 for three hours on the lake.

"Cranes? Yes, there are plenty around – you'll find them on Caohai"

25

10 Cruising the Three Gorges

There's something about China that's constantly cutting you down to size: the density of the crowds, the five thousand years of history, the complexity of the language, the awkwardness of chopsticks... But often it's the scenery alone, no more so than at Qutang Gorge, the first and most ferocious of the famous Three Gorges that together flank a 300-kilometre-long stretch of the Yangzi. "A thousand seas poured into one teacup" was how the poet Su Dongpo described this narrow, steep-sided canyon – though that was before the river had been domesticated by the dynamite and dams that have cleared hidden shoals, raised water levels and slowed the flow. Yet it's not to be scoffed at even today, and you won't find much excuse to hide in your cabin for the duration of the three-day cruise between Chongqing and Hubei provinces (not that a spartan four square metres of lumpy mattress and blocked toilet costing the price of a three-star hotel room is any competition). The landscape might be humbling but it also demands to be admired. The best of it isn't on the Yangzi but the offshoot Daning River, through the Little Three Gorges – a cool stretch of lime-blue water with monkeys and prehistoric coffins hanging from perpendicular cliffs. But where to attach superlatives? The Wu Gorge, framed by mountains which drop sheer from their peaks to the water? Or Xiling Gorge, seventy-six kilometres of cliffs with names like Ox Liver or Horse Lung? Or the final, man-made obstruction, the 1983-metre-long, 185-metre-high Three Gorges Dam – which, this being China, is naturally the largest in the world.

Practicalities

Passenger boats run year-round through the Three Gorges, though spring and autumn provide the most colourful scenery. Public ferries with basic cabins cost ¥1022 per person for the three-day run from Chongqing to Yichang; food is very simple so bring your own. Tour boats with hotel-like facilities charge ¥4000 for the same trip. Side tours and entry to historic sites along the way are not covered in the fares; the Little Three Gorges costs ¥150 and lasts four hours. Public ferry tickets are sold at the Yangzi Ferry Ticket Office on Shaanxi Lu, Chaotianmen docks, Chongqing; tour boat berths are best booked through an agent before leaving home, or with online agents such as ⓦwww. chinahighlights.com.

11
Getting beaten at Wudang Shan

If in travels around China you hope to find a place where **bearded mystics totter around mountain temples** in between performing amazing feats of martial prowess, then head for **Wudang Shan (the Martial Mountain)** in Hubei province. Mythologized versions of this place can be seen in big-screen martial arts epics such as **Crouching Tiger, Hidden Dragon**, which made such a big impression in the West; if domestic critical response was more muted, it's only because people here were already used to this sort of thing. But there's no doubt that kungfu is a growth industry in modern China, not least because of the **need for security**: crime rates have mirrored the explosion in personal wealth with today's more capitalist-driven, free-market society, and the demand for **bodyguards** has increased alongside. Students can study **kungfu** privately, at **martial art academies** (where many hope to become **film stars**), and even at Wudang Shan, which is one of the homes of traditional Chinese kungfu.

There is a catch, however. Firstly, to study full-time at one of Wudang's temples you have to become a **Taoist monk**, which – what with the accompanying **sexual abstinence**, spartan living conditions and **religious doctrine** – might not appeal. Secondly, these people are serious. Not necessarily vicious, but you'll have to get used to being **hit with fists**, fingers, palms, feet, sticks and and an escalating number of weapons. Turn up casually, however, and you'll probably find people willing to spend an hour or two teaching you some basics of their systems without involving too much hand-to-hand combat. And even if you're not in the slightest bit interested in getting into a scrap, the **mountain and its temples** are a rare treat, with stone paths rising through thin woodland to the magnificent sight of the mountain's summit completely ringed by a **fortress-like stone wall**, a group of gold- and green-tiled temples rising within.

Practicalities

Wudang Shan is in northwestern Hubei; from the nearest train station at Shiyan (25km west), catch a bus to Wudang town at the bottom of the mountain and then a minibus to Nanyan temple, about halfway up (¥20 in total). Entry to the mountain is ¥75, with extra entry fees for the various temples along the way. A tiring two-hour track leads from Nanyan to the summit. The best temple to see martial arts being performed at is Zixiao Gong, a half-hour walk downhill from Nanyan temple.

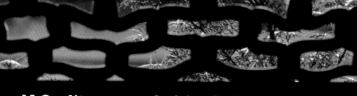

12 Quality space: admiring Suzhou's gardens

Since the thirteenth century, even Westerners have known about the cultured city of Suzhou, after Marco Polo wrote of its skilful artisans and sages in his book of travels. Incredibly, it still occupies an elevated position in the modern Chinese psyche: a popular saying lists Suzhou's virtues as its beautiful women, silk, and – especially – gardens, the design of which dates back over a thousand years to the Song dynasty.

Polo probably never saw one, however; far from being for the enjoyment of the masses, gardens were attached to family mansions, designed by wealthy merchants and scholars as private, contemplative retreats. Most pack a lot of detail into a very small space, and their construction was a genuine art, using carefully positioned rocks, pools, walls, windows and trees to create a sense of balance, harmony and proportion, where literature could be studied or a friend entertained over a cup of wine.

Well, that was the original idea, but holding on to any such lofty notions today is asking to be crushingly disappointed by the daily hordes of tourists that pack out these delicate, interlinked courtyards. Get around a few, however – about ten are open to the public – and you'll still pick up on echoes of what they were originally planned for, though the famous and complementary Wangshi Yuan (best viewed in moonlight), Shizi Lin with its naturally shaped rocks, and watery Zhuozheng Yuan are constantly seething with people. If you're lucky and get in first thing in the morning before others arrive, however, you might even find a few minutes to yourself at the relatively unknown Canglang Ting and Ou Yuan gardens, and maybe catch just a glimpse of a more refined time.

Practicalities

Suzhou is in eastern China, about 50km west of Shanghai. The gardens are scattered through the centre of town, though you'll need taxis if you plan to visit a lot of them in one day. Entry fees for the gardens are ¥10–50, and they open daily from around 7.30am to 4.30pm. Tours and guides can be arranged through your hotel, or with CITS, Dajing Xiang (☎0512/65155207).

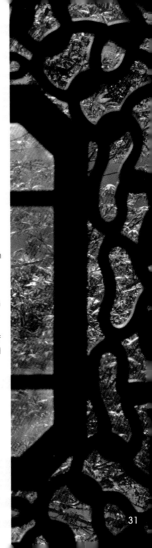

13 Meeting pandas at Wolong, Sichuan

It's not everywhere that you can open your eyes and see a measurable percentage of a species' entire population in one go. But you can at Wolong, in western Sichuan province, founded in 1975 as the first of China's half-dozen reserves to specifically protect the giant panda. Numbers are sketchy, but certainly less than fifteen hundred survive, even including captive animals, and yet at Wolong's research centre you can find yourself looking at them twenty at a time.

Not that there is much to see at first. Pandas live mostly on bamboo (with a little carrion as relish now and again), which doesn't pack a sufficient calorific punch for an overly active lifestyle. Unless they're courting or eating – and it's not as if bamboo needs much effort to sneak up on even then – pandas tend to lead a pretty quiet existence. All twenty of them are likely to doze through your visit, mostly wedged into the forks of shady trees.

So why come to Wolong, if you can experience pretty much the same thing at your local zoo? Especially since you've almost no chance of seeing wild pandas here, as their population is too thinly spread and their alpine forest habitat is just too impenetrable to explore. But then your local zoo doesn't have the mountains that pandas actually live in as its backdrop. You haven't just spent four hours bouncing uphill in a bus from the provincial capital, Chengdu, to this narrow valley, with its brilliant snowy peaks looming above and Tibetans herding yaks by the roadside. Nor have you stood waiting impatiently for just one of the pandas to actually wake up and do something, when the idea has struck that up there in the hills – just where you're looking perhaps – this rare animal survives in its natural state.

Practicalities

Buses to Wolong (several daily, ¥31) leave early in the morning from Chadianzi bus station out in Chengdu's northwestern outskirts, at the end of the #81 bus route.

Cracking the ice festival, Harbin

Getting out and about when the **temperature dips to forty below** may seem a little crazy, but that doesn't stop the thousands of visitors who every January don thick coats, **hats and gloves** and head to Harbin, capital of the wintery, northeastern province of Heilongjiang. That's when **an army of builders** from China, Russia, Europe, Asia and even Australia descend on the city, fire up their chainsaws, axes and chisels and kick off Harbin's month-long Winter Ice Festival by carving out **all sorts of extraordinary sculptures** in the city's parks from ice blocks cut from the **Songhua River**.

A surreal cityscape of cathedrals, pyramids, Thai palaces and Chinese temples rises in Zhaolin Park, most of the replicas built to scale but so large you can actually wander through them, though some – including a section of the Great Wall, which inevitably puts in an appearance – are life-sized. And as if a parkful of transparent, fairytale castles wasn't enough, at night everything is lit up splendidly in lurid colours by light bulbs embedded in the ice, drawing huge crowds despite the intense cold. Across the Songhua River, Sun Island is another park populated this time by snow sculptures. A few of these follow traditional Chinese themes (you'll usually find a giant Guanyin, the Buddhist incarnation of mercy), but most are more contemporary cartoon characters, overblown mythical creatures or fantastical inhabitants of the sculptor's mind. And then amongst these are straightforward busts of famous Americans, or just a life-sized sculpture of a horse, which – amongst such bizarre companions – pull you up by their very ordinariness.

Practicalities

You can reach Harbin from Beijing by train (9 daily; 17hr) or plane (13 daily; 1hr 30min). The Winter Ice Festival (¥30) officially lasts from January 5 until February 5, though recent years have seen it extended until March.

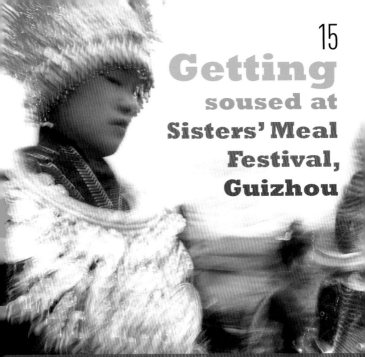

Getting
soused at
Sisters' Meal
Festival,
Guizhou

Practicalities

Sisters' Meal Festival lasts three days and takes place in and around
Taijiang town, which can be reached on plentiful buses (¥15, 90min) daily
from Kaili city in eastern Guizhou. Accommodation in Taijiang is limited to
simple guesthouses charging around ¥30 per person for a double room
with shared bathroom. The festival's dates are calculated using the lunar
calendar, and so change each year, but it's usually some time in April.
A useful local contact is CITS in Kaili (daily 8.30–11.30am & 2.30–6pm,
☎0855/8222506, ⓦwww.qdncits.com), who can advise on exact dates,
book accommodation and provide guides.

"Make him do it again!" This from a young policeman who had just missed his chance to photograph me spilling about a pint of home-made rice wine down my front. **For the second time.** Well, it's not every day that you get carjacked by a score of beautiful girls dressed in exquisitely **embroidered silk jackets** and enough silverware to sink a battleship, and forced to quaff from a **buffalo-horn's worth of raw spirit** if you want to carry on your way. **"Don't touch the horn"** warned a friend, "or you'll have to drain it!" So I stood with my hands behind my back while one of the girls held up the wine and tried to get me to sip. But **buffalo-horn goblets** are obviously not designed for Westerners – a mouthful went in, but my big nose bumped the edge, and my shirt got the rest. **The crowd loved it.**

Such are the hazards of attending the Miao people's Sisters' Meal Festival at Shidong, Guizhou province, the time of the year when **all marriageable girls** from the local villages **pick a husband**. This was the third and final day, by which time I'd already got involved in vigorous group dances, had **fireworks** thrown at me (nothing personal – just part of the action) during a riotous late-night **dragon-lantern competition**, and narrowly missed being trampled by the loser at a buffalo-wrestling contest. Now all twenty thousand participants were heading to a nearby river to wind the festival up with some **dragon-boat races**. The roadblock was passed at last, but not before the **policeman had got his photos**, I'd sunk a skinful, and the world had become decidedly **fuzzy around the edges**. All I can remember is that after the boat races, all twenty thousand of us formed rings and **danced and sang until dawn**. At least, that's what my head felt like I'd done the next morning.

16 On foot through Tiger Leaping Gorge

"A stony path winds up to cool hills", or so goes a Chinese poem. Well, it was never truer than where a youthful Yangzi channels violently through Tiger Leaping Gorge in Yunnan province, the stony path in question winding up to the foothills of an ash-grey, spiky range – though the peaks, at over 5000m high, spoil the comparison by actually being mountains. Of course, poetry also doesn't mention anything as mundane as what it's like to lug a backpack around for three days at this altitude: rather tiring. Nor does it explain the 100-metre-wide gorge's name. After asking a handful of villagers, you'll suspect that you might not be the first idiot who has quizzed them about it: "A tiger was being chased, and it leaped across the river to escape" is their well-rehearsed answer.

Altitude and names aside though, trekking through the gorge is fantastic. The Chinese don't usually have a romantic view of nature,

rather they see the Great Outdoors as being frighteningly empty, unless livened up by tour groups, cable cars, stone staircases, strategically placed pavilions, souvenir hawkers and noodle stands. But here there is nothing – just the mountains, the path, the gorge and a huge, blue sky. Occasionally you'll see a farmer or some goats; every few hours' walking throws up a couple of houses. You sleep along the way at small villages, and can sit outside under a gloriously luminous Milky Way while an unlikely number of satellites race in straight lines across the night.

Practicalities

Tiger Leaping Gorge (¥30) is 70km north of Lijiang town, in northwestern Yunnan. Buses run daily from Lijiang to the endpoints at easterly Daju and westerly Qiaotou (3hr; ¥20). The full trek takes at least two days, though three is recommended; you need to be fairly fit and shouldn't hike alone. Spring and autumn are the best months for walking as summer can be very wet, with potentially dangerous landslides.

strolling the
Shanghai Bund

If Europeans ever made a real impact on China it was in the part they played in turning interwar Shanghai into one of the busiest, raciest cities in the world. Haunt of aristocrats, businessmen, gangsters and untold millions of beggars, prostitutes and day-labourers who barely managed to scrape together their daily bowl of rice, Shanghai through the 1920s and 30s was almost a caricature of itself – and also why the city was deliberately run down by the Chinese Communist government that took over in 1949. Today, however, Shanghai is booming again, with a growth in hyper-modern architecture and commercial dealings which is beginning to offer serious competition to its long-term rival and fellow former colonial construction, Hong Kong.

And yet it's still one of old Shanghai's landmarks that is used as a benchmark of how the city is changing. Running south along the west bank of the Huangpu River for a couple of kilometres, the road known as the Bund was once Shanghai's docks and commercial heart in one, lined with European neo-classical warehouses, banks and expensive hotels, some of which survive amongst the modern cityscape. Walking south, you pass the former British and Russian consulates and waterside Huangpu Park, infamous for signs once allegedly barring "dogs or Chinese" and now one of the best places to promenade and watch the latest high-tech developments springing up over the river at Pudong district. Further on are the one-time headquarters of Jardine Matheson (which made its original fortune in the opium trade) and the art-deco Peace Hotel, known as the Cathay Hotel through the 1930s when its jazz band was the talk of the town. Incredibly, some of the musicians' descendants still provide a nightly show. Beyond here are the Bank of China, Customs House (still functioning), the Hong Kong and Shanghai Bank (HSBC), and Dongfeng Hotel, once the men-only Shanghai Club whose 33-metre-long mahogany bar is sadly no more. Wind up your walk nearby with a meal at M On The Bund, where the views (if not the Mediterranean-style food) are outstanding.

Practicalities

The Bund (known in Chinese as Zhongshan Dong Lu or Wai Tan) is south of Suzhou Creek on the western bank of the Huangpu River, central Shanghai.

18 Step aerobics: climbing Huang Shan

Practicalities

To reach Huang Shan you first need to take a train, bus or plane to Tunxi, 50km southwest, and then a minibus from there to accommodation at the mountain's base at Tangkou (many daily; ¥13). Further minibus taxis run on demand from Tangkou up the mountain to the start of hiking trails at Ciguang Ge or Yungu Si. The Ciguang Ge trail takes around eight hours and has the best scenery; the Yungu Si route takes three but you see very little. Once at the summit area, it takes around three hours to circuit the peaks. There are four hotels around the summit; dormitory beds cost ¥150 and double rooms at least ¥600. A cable car runs the entire Yungu Si route (¥85 each way) so could be used for the descent.

The Chinese would say that *"where there is yin, there is yang"*; Westerners would more prosaically opine *"no gain without pain"*. At Huang Shan, Anhui province's Yellow Mountains, this means *ravishing scenery* tempered by *steps, steps and more steps*. All fifteen kilometres of the path to the top of Huang Shan is cut into steps and paved in stone, which has been quarried, carried up here and laid by hand in an *amazing human endeavour*. Incidentally, it has also made the mountain accessible to generations of the country's greatest painters and poets, whose impressions have turned Huang Shan into a national icon of natural beauty, today drawing the *inevitable cartloads of footstepping tourists*. The mountain's procession of clouds, *soaring granite monoliths* and wind-contorted pine trees are at first like being in a Chinese garden writ large, but you soon realize that the experience of being here is what those gardens' designers were trying to capture and fit into some rich patron's backyard, where it could be appreciated without the need for having to do *eight hours of step aerobics*.

Unsurprisingly, the reality is not quite the same. You can come in winter, when there are very few people and the mountain is *overlaid with another layer of grandeur*, but it's far easier to enjoy spring or autumn – colourful times when nature is in transition. The crowds are worse (though not as bad as they are during summer), but at least you have someone to share your pain with while gasping ever upwards. Yet the toughest moment of all is on reaching the "top", only to find *there's no real summit* to stand on, rather *a plateau ringed in little peaks* which bring Huang Shan's height to within a whisker of 1900m. The finest sight here is watching as the sun rises from or sets into a cloud sea, while sharing the experience with hundreds of other onlookers, *all momentarily hushed by the spectacle.*

With its faintly Mediterranean atmosphere, what better place to while away a warm summer day than Beidaihe, on the coast just a few hours fom Beijing?

There was once a time when foreigners in China were the only people with a handle on beach life, and the Chinese would sit in uncomfortable family groups, ill at ease in their bathing gear, clearly worried about wading out of their depth in the water, and looking as if they knew that it should all be fun, but wondering how to go about it. China's non-steroid-enhanced swim team's performance at the 2004 Olympic Games in Athens swept all that away. Now, fired by national pride, the water beckons the athletic, while the less-competitive remainder parade in their surprisingly skimpy swimsuits, lounge on the sand, or play beachball between the huge granite statues of heroic workers which once set the political tone. Most people here are ordinary, aspiring youngsters and nouveaux riches from Beijing, though the occasional cruising black Audi with dark windows harks back to a time when the sand and surf were reserved for the sole enjoyment of the party elite. Back along the promenade, shops sell exactly the sort of seaside kitsch you'd expect from the setting (fluorescent swimsuits, animal sculptures made of seashells), while private villas of the rich sport ludicrously overblown architectural flourishes. The best places to hang out, once you've had enough of the beach, are the many excellent restaurants, where you can down a cold beer and make your choice from seafood so fresh that it's still flapping around in a bucket.

19 Beach lounging at Beidaihe

Practicalities

Beidaihe is on the east China coast, about 2hr 30min from Beijing by train (7 daily). The beaches stretch for around 5km along the south side of a broad peninsula, easily walkable from town or reached on buses #6 or #34. The beach season lasts from late spring through to early autumn.

20 The ride of your life:
by bus to Dêgê

Bored with western Sichuan's pandas, pristine blue lakes, raw mountain scenery and Tibetan monasteries? Well then, for what is likely to prove one of the most adrenaline-packed eight hours of your life, **ride the public bus from Ganzi to Dêgê.** You start already 3500 metres up in a river valley at the foot of the Que'er Shan range, Ganzi's dusty sprawl of tiled concrete buildings disappearing abruptly around a corner behind you, the bus packed to capacity with raucous crowds of Tibetans. The road – like all roads here if you're riding west towards the Himalayan Plateau – heads ever upwards, crossing a wide pass **festooned with bright prayer flags** at the head of the valley, at which point the Tibetans all cheer and hurl handfuls of paper prayers out the windows like clouds of confetti. Beyond is the halfway town of Manigange, where the passengers get out and (despite their Buddhist leanings) **consume vast quantities of meat dumplings and butter tea** – the latter revolting as tea but satisfying if thought of as soup. Back into the bus, past brown glaciers hemming in the holy lake of Yilhun Lhatso and boulders carved in Tibetan script with "Om Mani Padme Hum", and the valley reaches a rounded conclusion beneath some particularly wicked-looking, spiky, snow-bound peaks. Unfortunately, the road goes on, winding back on itself as it climbs up… and up… and up. The Tibetans are no longer so boisterous; several are **blatantly chanting prayers**, thumbing rosaries with their eyes screwed up tight. Up amongst the peaks now, and the bus is suddenly **rocked by winds as the road wobbles** through the narrow, 5050-metre-high pass and around a corner so tight that at night you'd be over the edge before you even knew that there was a corner to turn. On the far side, the road slaloms down a virtually vertical rockface to the valley far below, and then it's an unadventurous run to Dêgê, just an hour away.

The Chinese don't look for a quiet, romantic, candle-lit ambience in their restaurants. No, for them the hallmark of a great eating experience is bright lights, the happy chatter of satisfied customers stuffing their faces, and an atmosphere best described as *renao* – "hot and noisy" – and it would be hard to imagine a hotter, noisier restaurant than Liwan Mingshijia at 99 Dishifu Lu, Guangzhou (aka Canton). It's small – just a single room – but the benches and heavy wood-and-marble tables are so closely packed that *the waitresses have a tough time getting close* enough to deliver your meal, which only adds to the chaotic environment. No chance of getting a table to yourself either; you're forced to cheerfully jog elbows and spill tea over your neighbours, who will probably be curious to find out whether, as a foreigner, you can use chopsticks and what you've ordered to eat. This is, crudely speaking, a traditional-style *dim sum* house, serving lots of little dishes of dumplings, soups, cakes and savouries to be eaten with tea. The menu is hand-written item-by-item on scores of small wooden boards hung around the walls, which you have to decipher before pushing your way to the rear counter, placing your order, and getting back to your seat. The crowds here speak for the food being fantastic, and it is: highlights are *sheung fan*, paper-thin steamed rice-noodle sheets scattered with prawns and rolled up; cones of sticky rice wrapped in lotus leaves and stuffed with chicken and bamboo; and unusual *tang yuan* (rice-flour balls), filled with red bean paste and served in a sweet soup flavoured with medicinal lily bulbs. And the cost of a meal for four, including excellent *tie guanyin* tea – just twelve yuan (around £1) a head.

You're forced to cheerfully jog elbows and spill tea over your neighbours, who will probably be curious to find out whether, as a foreigner, you can use chopsticks.

Practicalities

Liwan Mingshijia, 99 Dishifu Lu, in western-central Guangzhou. Opens around 8am-8pm daily. No English spoken, or English menus; if you can't speak or read Chinese, grab a waitress, have a look at what others are eating and point to what looks good.

Horsing about in **Inner** Mongolia

If China's urban crowds, grey skies, noise and pollution start getting under your skin, it's time to head north of the Great Wall to Inner Mongolia, land of Genghis Khan and his people, who exploded out of their homelands to conquer half the known world on horseback and a diet of fermented mares' milk and raw meat, tenderized by keeping it under the saddle. Under Genghis' grandson Kublai Khan, the Mongols ruled China for a century from 1271 (a period witnessed first-hand by Marco Polo), before a popular rebellion threw them out and back over the Wall to a life of petty tribal squabbling.

Modern Mongolia is not one vast prairie prowled by hairy horsemen, but there certainly are parts of it where the rolling grasslands grazed by sheep and horses seem to go on indefinitely and there's a chance to see some traditional Mongol life – or the tourist version of it, at any rate. The most visited areas surround the provincial capital, Hohhot, at Xilamuren, Gegentala and Huitengxile, where there are well-established camps of yurts, large Mongolian felt tents with a central fireplace and floored with rugs. Visitors get well-rehearsed entertainments laid on by a cast in full national costume, including wrestling matches and shows of astounding horsemanship, the riders performing acrobatic feats at full pelt. Late-night bouts imbibing cups of local raw spirits, leading to unabashed singing and dancing sessions, are probably just as authentic but feel a tad degenerate. Less accessible grasslands such as Hulunbuir near the town of Hailar might offer a more authentic experience, as the people here still herd for a living, rather than relying on the tourist dollar. Either area, however, lies well outside the usual image of China, and truly getting away on your own is as easy as hiring a horse for the day and aiming for the horizon.

Practicalities

Hohhot is connected to Beijing by plane (5 daily; 1hr 10min) and train (12 daily; 10hr). All-inclusive two-day tours to Xilamuren, Gegentala or Huitengxile grasslands (80–120km from Hohhot) cost ¥250–350 per person in a group of six; a recommended operator is Inner Mongolia International Travel Company at Hohot's *Tongda* hotel (☎0471/6968613). You can also reach Xilamuren independently by bus from Hohhot to Zhaohe (2 buses daily; 2–3hr; ¥8) and then negotiate a night in a yurt with touts at the bus station (about ¥50 per person including food). The best time to visit is late spring through to late summer; outside these times the weather is too cold.

23 The Mother of all Markets

They call it the "Mother of all Markets", and so they should: every week, one hundred thousand nomads, villagers and traders from all over central Asia converge on Kashgar, the last sizeable place you'll come to in China if you're heading northwest along the ancient Silk Road. They're here to take part in the Yekshenba Bazaar, the Sunday Market, which fills the teahouses and dusty lanes of this Muslim city with a blur of noise and smells that went out of fashion elsewhere in the world after the Middle Ages. Ground zero is a trampled area to the east of the city, where customers and traders haggle with melodramatic flair over the merits of horses, sheep, camels and donkeys. Just when it seems as if someone is about to get a knife in the ribs, the shouting and fist-shaking gives way to satisfied nods, money changes hands, and the new owner leads his purchases away. Beyond all this horse-trading is the covered market, a maze of shaded stalls better-stocked than a Western shopping mall, whose owners sip tea, chat with their friends, and do their best to catch your eye so that they can beckon you over. They are masters of soft-sell; each in their friendly, persuasive way makes it hard to escape without buying something. "Need some kitchenware – a new cleaver, some pots and pans? No problem, I have these. How about a carpet? This one, from Khotan, perhaps – or how about a fine kilim, handmade by nomads? Some Iranian saffron then; yes, more expensive than gold. A pity to come so far and leave empty-handed." But where to start – over here are musical instruments, wooden chests inlaid with tin (used for carrying gifts to prospective brides), and enough food to last a lifetime – where to start?

Practicalities

Kashgar's Yekshenba Bazaar takes place every Sunday about 2km from the city centre off Ayziret Lu; it's best to walk there as the crowds make it difficult to reach by taxi. It kicks off early on in the day, reaches a peak by late morning and is beginning to slow noticeably by mid-afternoon. The greatest variety of traders are here between May and October, when the Pakistan border is open.

53

The Great Wall is one of those sights that you've seen and heard so much about that you know reality is going to have a tough time living up to the hype. But having made it all the way to Beijing, it seems perverse to ignore this overblown landmark, so arm yourself with a thermos of tea and catch a bus north from the capital to Simatai, one of several sections of this 4800-kilometre-long structure which has been restored.

24
Blown
away
at the
Great Wall

It's easy to find bad things to say about the Great Wall. The work of China's megalomaniac first emperor Qin Shi Huang, over a million forced labourers are said to have died building the original around 250 BC, and the simple truth is that this seven-metre-high, seven-metre-thick barrier didn't even work. History is littered with "barbarian" invaders who proved sophisticated enough to fight or bribe their way around the wall's 25,000 watch-towers, most notably the Mongols in the thirteenth century, and the Manchus – who went on to become China's final dynasty – in 1644. Indeed, the Manchus were so unimpressed with the wall that they let the entire thing fall into ruin.

And yet, you'll be blown away. Not even swarms of hawkers and other tourists can ruin the sight of this blue-grey ribbon snaking across the dusty, shattered hills into the hazy distance, beyond which one end finally runs into the sea, while the other simply stops in northwestern China's deserts. You can spend hours walking between battlements along the top – in places following the contours of the hills up amazing inclines – until restorations give way to rubble, and even then you can't quite believe that such a solid, organic part of the scenery is only an artefact, built by simple human endeavour. If ever proof were needed of Chinese determination, this is it.

Practicalities

Many sections of the Great Wall are accessible as a day-trip from Beijing, including heavily touristed Badaling (daily 9am–4.30pm, ¥35), 70km northwest; less visited Mutianyu (daily 8am–4pm, ¥35) 90km northeast; and atmospheric Simatai (daily 8am–4pm, ¥32). Most Beijing hotels run tours, though these tend to be expensive, or you can catch local buses: tourist bus #1 and #5 to Badaling (daily 6–10am, ¥50) from Qianmen Dong Dajie; tourist bus #6 from Xuanwumen to Mutianyu (April 15–Oct 15 7–8.30am, ¥45); tourist bus #12 from opposite Xuanwumen Metro stop to Simitai (mid-April–mid-Oct 6–8am, ¥50). Journey times are from 90min to 3hr each way.

25 Taking tea in Chengdu

China is a busy place and the Chinese are a busy people, not overly given to spending time that could be spent on making money sitting idly around in public. Which is why many Chinese from other provinces consider the Sichuanese – particularly those from Chengdu – inherently lazy. They're not, they just like their local culture, and have filled just about every available public space, from temple gardens to pavements alongside busy roads, with teahouses. Actually, calling most of these places "teahouses" is a bit grand: they can be just a humble cluster of plastic tables and chairs, though the best look like something from a Chinese film set, all medieval curly roofs, wooden screens and wobbly bamboo furniture around which waiters navigate with stacks of porcelain cups and kettles of hot water.

Practicalities

Two of Chengdu's busiest teahouses are at Renmin Park in the city centre, and Wenshu Temple, 1.5km north off Renmin Zhong Lu. Both open daily from dawn to dusk, but are liveliest at the weekends. A cup of standard jasmine tea costs ¥5, zhuye qing around ¥10; refills are free.

All around are comfortably sociable groups reading newspapers, playing mahjong, staring off into space with cheroots between their teeth or chatting to friends. Really ambitious establishments even offer light meals, though it's not really what people are here for – in a country where it's usually so hard to relax in public, teahouses are a welcome escape.

Ultimate experiences
China
miscellany

 **Food**

China has four major cuisines: southern (mild and fresh flavours); eastern (sweet and oily); western (hot and spicy); and northern (rich and pickled). Rice is the staple only in southern China; elsewhere wheat buns or noodles are preferred.

▶▶ 5 foods to try

- Beijing Roast Duck
- Cantonese dim sum (aka yum cha)
- Mapo toufu (spicy beancurd)
- Dongpo rouding (steamed belly pork)
- Jiaozi (crescent-shaped steamed or fried dumplings, a bit like ravioli and a great staple all over the country)

Restaurant bills are not shared out among the guests but instead people will go to great lengths to claim the honour of paying the whole bill by themselves. Normally that honour will fall to the person perceived as the most senior, and as a foreigner dining with Chinese you should make some effort to stake your claim, though it is probable that someone else will grab the bill before you do. Attempting to pay a "share" of the bill may cause serious embarrassment.

▶▶ 5 great restaurants

Long Chaoshou in Chengdu, Sichuan. Chaotic, renowned dumpling house.

Liwan Mingshijia in Guangzhou, Guangdong. Ming-style canteen and teahouse serving dim-sum-style snacks.

Huo Dian (Fire Palace) in Changsha, Hunan. Riotously good Hunanese food.

Qianmen Quanjude Roast Duck in Beijing. A Beijing institution.

1221 in Shanghai. Creative Shanghainese cuisine.

Technology

One in four people in China owns a **mobile phone** – around 325 million people.

China has over 110 million Internet users – less than 9% of China's population, but already the world's second biggest online population after the US.

 # Chinese medicine

Traditional Chinese medicine works by balancing the body's flow of qi, or vital energy, which can become interrupted by illness. Interruption causes deficiency or excess of yin or yang principles, which are balanced using tonic "herbs" (including plant and animal parts); while acupuncture uses fine needles to stimulate or reduce the flow of qi around relevant parts of the body.

Cinema

▶▶ China on film

A Chinese Ghost Story (1987). One of the seminal Hong Kong films of the 1980s – part horror film, part love story, part martial arts blockbuster.

Beijing Bastards (1993). One of the best of China's "underground movies".

Crouching Tiger, Hidden Dragon (2000). Epic martial arts film that was a massive hit in the West.

Blind Shaft (2003). Deemed too controversial for domestic release – a telling indictment of runaway capitalism and a great piece of film noir.

Kung Fu Hustle (2004). A melange of surreal comedy, pastiche, slapstick and kung fu.

Religion

There are two major religions in China: indigenous **Taoism**, which seeks to understand the natural structure of all things; and **Buddhism**, imported from India in the second century and believing in gradual spiritual enlightenment over the course of successive lives. Overlying these is **Confucianism**, a moral philosophy formulated around 500 BC and teaching respect based on rigid social order, which is deeply rooted in the Chinese psyche irrespective of the nominal religion followed.

▸▸ Top 5 religious sites

Temple of Heaven, Beijing. Classic Ming-dynasty building.
Dafo (Great Buddha), Leshan, Sichuan. The largest Buddhist sculpture in the world.
Potala Palace, Lhasa. Enduring landmark of Tibet's foremost city.
Yungang Caves, Datong. Glorious fifth-century Buddhist statuary.
Tai Shan, Shandong. Holy mountain famed for its magnificent scenery and temples.

6 Space

During the 1960s Chairman Mao lamented that China could not "even get a potato into orbit". In 2003 China became the third nation (along with Russia and the US) to successfully launch a manned spacecraft. China now plans to send an unmanned probe to the moon by 2012, possibly with Russian assistance.

"With time and patience the mulberry leaf becomes a silk gown"

Chinese proverb

Transport

China has over 73,000km of rail track, including a new route to Tibet – the highest rail line in the world – which reaches an altitude of 5072m as it crosses the Himalayan Plateau. The carriages on this line have to be pressurized like an aircraft because of the altitude.

"A journey of a thousand miles begins with a single step"

Chinese proverb

 # History

Chinese Dynasties

Xia 21C–16C BC
Shang 16C–11C BC
Zhou 11C–221 BC
Qin 221–207 BC
Han 206 BC–220 AD
Three Kingdoms 200–280
Jin 265–420
Sixteeen Kingdoms 420–581
Sui 581–618
Tang 618–907
Five Dynasties 907–960
Song 960–1271
Yuan 1271–1368
Ming 1368–1644
Qing 1644–1911
....
Republic of China 1911–1949
People's Republic of China 1949–present

China's **first emperor** was Qin Shihuang, who unified what had been a group of warring states in 221 BC. The **last emperor** was Aisin Gioro Pu Yi, who abdicated in favour of a republican government in 1912. Between these two ruled 157 emperors of eight major dynasties. The only emperor popularly known by name in the West is Kublai Khan of the Yuan (Mongol) dynasty, who died in 1294.

The **Silk Road** was the trade route running northwest out of China into Central Asia, along which Buddhism was first imported to China and silk first exported to Europe. Established before 100 BC, trade reached a peak during the outward-looking Tang dynasty (618–907 AD), but eventually declined as China became more isolationist and faster maritime routes were charted.

 **9 Martial arts**

Most Chinese martial arts trace their histories back to the Shaolin Temple in Henan province, where the sixth-century Buddhist monk Bodhidharma first developed kungfu routines as exercises to balance the long hours spent in meditation. Popular martial arts styles include Shaolin kungfu, tai chi, bagua zhang, mantis kungfu, xingyi quan, wing chun, white crane and choi li fut.

10 Hotels

▶▶ **5 great hotels**

Mandarin Oriental, Central, Hong Kong. Excellent service, prime location and a great place to people watch.

The Peninsula, Tsim Sha Tsui, Hong Kong. Among the world's classiest hotels, overlooking the harbour.

St Regis, Jianguomen Wai Dajie, Beijing. The best and most expensive hotel in the city.

Peace Hotel, Shanghai. Perhaps Shanghai's most famous grand, old-world hotel.

Grand Hyatt Pudong, Shanghai. Occupies the top 36 floors of one of the world's tallest buildings.

Tea

Tea has been drunk in China for at least three thousand years. There are three types, depending on how the leaves are processed: green tea, where the leaves are picked and dried directly; black tea, where the leaves are fermented before being dried; and oolong tea, which is semi-fermented.

12 Literature

▸▸ Books on China

The Judge Dee Mysteries by Robert Van Gulik. Sherlock Holmes-style detective stories set in the Tang dynasty.

River Town by Peter Hessler. One of the best of the mini-genre "how I taught English for a couple of years in China and survived".

Mr China by Tim Clissold. Eye-opening story of how the author went to China in 1988 to make a fortune and lost 400 million dollars.

The Seige at Peking by Peter Fleming. Account of the siege in 1900, which lasted 55 days and led to a watershed in China's relations with the rest of the world.

Chinese Food by Kenneth Lo. Includes Westernized dishes as well as regional specialities.

▸▸ Chinese literature

Romance of the Three Kingdoms by Luo Guanzhong. One of the world's great historical novels, covering the turbulent Three Kingdoms period.

Journey to the West by Wu Cheng'en. Absurd, lively rendering of the Buddhist monk Xuanzang's pilgrimage to India.

The Analects by Confucius. Collection of teachings on morality and the state.

The Art of War by Sun Zi. A classic dating back to 500 BC and still popular with the business community today.

Shanghai Baby by Wei Hui. Chinese chick-lit.

13 Sport

Soccer and **basketball** are the most popular sports in China. The national football team made it to the World Cup in 2002, and Chinese national Yao Ming is a star of the US National Basketball Association.

14 Politics

China's sole political organization is the Chinese Communist Party, with a President (State Head) and Premier (Head of Government). The country enjoys "communism with Chinese characteristics", essentially a free-market economy but with no room for political dissent against the Party.

"Great souls have wills; feeble ones have only wishes"

Chinese proverb

The **Cultural Revolution** (1964–76) was an attempt by China's leader, Chairman Mao, to dismantle traditional society by organizing a nationwide youth militia (the Red Guard) to burn books, destroy historical monuments and humiliate or execute anyone who clung to the old order.

15 Habits and etiquette

Chinese have almost no concept of **privacy**. People will stare at each other from point-blank range and pluck letters or books out of others' hands for close inspection. Even toilets are built with partitions so low that you can chat with your neighbour while squatting.

Smoking is almost universal among men and any attempt to stop others from lighting up is met with incomprehension. Handing out cigarettes is a basic way of establishing goodwill and non-smokers should be apologetic about turning down offered cigarettes.

Average number of manufactured cigarettes smoked per man per day in China

1952........................1
1972........................4
1992........................10
1996........................15

Outside the company of urban sophisticates, it would not occur to people that there was anything disrespectful in delivering a powerful **spit** while in conversation with a stranger – spitting can be observed in buses, trains, restaurants and even inside people's homes.

Inventions

Amongst many other things, the Chinese invented gunpowder, block printing, moveable type, the magnetic compass, iron ploughheads, the wheelbarrow, paper money, porcelain and woven silk.

Lucky symbols

Lucky colours in China are red and gold; **lucky numbers** are 3 and 8. White is the traditional colour of mourning, and the number 4 is considered unlucky since it sounds like the word for "dead". Car registration plates and telephone numbers with 3 and 8 in them are auctioned at high prices in Hong Kong. **Lucky symbols** include peaches and cranes (for longevity), fish (prosperity), mandarin ducks (marital fidelity), dragons (male power), phoenixes (female power) and bats (luck).

18 Natural environment

Highest mountains in China

Rank in world	mountain	height
1	Everest	8848m
2	K2	8611m
4	Makalu	8463m
5	Cho Oyu	8201m
11	Gasherbrum I	8068m

Eight out of the world's ten most **polluted cities** are in China. The causes are reliance on fossil fuels as a primary energy source, increasing traffic emissions, and untreated industrial waste.

Giant pandas are only found in the mountains of southwestern China, where they live on bamboo – a food source so low in nutrients that pandas spend at least twelve hours a day eating as much as 38 kilograms of it. Just 1200 pandas remain today, and the species is endangered, its survival threatened by habitat destruction.

▶▶ Top 5 natural attractions

Jiuzhaigou, Sichuan. One of China's most spectacular landscapes.

Flaming Mountains, Xinjiang. Stunning red sandstone hillsides.

Changbai Shan, Heilongjiang. The northeast's loveliest nature reserve.

Huang Shan, Anhui. Arguably China's most scenic mountain.

Zhangjiajie, Hunan. Mystical landscape of limestone towers.

19 Calligraphy

Calligraphy was crystallized into a high art form in China, valued on a par with painting. At one stage during the Tang dynasty, calligraphy was used as the yardstick for the selection of high officials.

There are a number of different calligraphy scripts: the **seal** script is the archaic form found on oracle bones; the **lishu** is the clerical style and was used in inscriptions on stone; the **kaishu** is the regular style closest to the modern printed form; and **cao shu** is the most individual hand-written style.

 # People

One consequence of the "one child" policy is that China is now one of the most **rapidly ageing** countries in the world. It is estimated that the proportion of those aged over 65 will increase from 7% of the population in 2000 to about 20% in 2040, and the very old – those aged over 80 – will increase from about 8 million to about 50 million.

Population of China

1949	540 million
1979	800 million
1995	1.23 billion
2006	1.31 billion
2025	1.49 billion (projected)

Language

Mandarin is China's national language, though scores of other languages and dialects are in regional use. Chinese languages are tonal, meaning that along with the pronunciation, the tone with which a word is spoken (for instance high, falling, or rising) completely changes its meaning: for instance the tones used saying "mai dan" mean you're either asking for the restaurant bill, or buying eggs.

Chinese writing is made up of over ten thousand characters, each representing a concept or single meaning. The oldest examples are carved on bones dated to 1600 BC and are simple pictograms; a few remaining in use today are recognizably pictorial but most have become abstract over the millennia.

22 Festivals

Festival	When and where
Spring Festival – family feasts, firecrackers and a lantern festival	▶▶ January/February; countrywide but best in Guangzhou and Hong Kong
Water Splashing Festival	▶▶ April 13–15; popular in Yunnan Province
Sisters' Meal Festival – dragon-lantern dances and buffalo fights	▶▶ April/May; Kaili, Guizhou Province
Cheung Chau Bun Festival – parades, opera performances and towers of sweet buns	▶▶ May; Hong Kong
Dragon-boat festival	▶▶ June/July; countrywide, though most famously at Yueyang in Hunan Province, and in Hong Kong
Moon Festival – family reunions, fireworks, lanterns and the eating of moon cakes	▶▶ September/October; countrywide
Confucius Festival	▶▶ September 28; celebrated at all Confucian temples

23 Shopping

▶▶ 5 souvenirs to buy

- DVDs and computer software.
- Reproduction porcelain antiques ("real" antiques tend not to be).
- Chinese tea – choose from hundreds of varieties.
- *The Little Red Book* by Chairman Mao Zedong, who coined the phrase "political power grows out of the barrel of a gun".
- Clothes – cheap and good quality.

"One cannot refuse to eat just because there is a chance of being choked"

Chinese proverb

24 Architecture

Four of the world's tallest buildings are in China: the Jin Mao Building, Shanghai (number 5; 421m); IFC2 Hong Kong (number 6; 415m); CITIC Plaza, Guangzhou (number 7; 391m); and Shun Hing Square, Shenzhen (number 8; 384m).

"Seeing it once is better than being told one hundred times"

Zhou Chongguo, Han Dynasty

25 **Astrology**

Chinese horoscope:

Animal	Year of birth (from Chinese New Year)	Characteristics
Rat	1936, 1948, 1960, 1972, 1984, 1996	generous, intelligent, insecure.
Ox	1937, 1949, 1961, 1973, 1985, 1997	obstinate, independent, conservative.
Tiger	1938, 1950, 1962, 1974, 1986, 1998	adventurous; creative, fearless.
Rabbit	1939, 1951, 1963, 1975, 1987, 1999	peace-loving, timid, long-lived.
Dragon	1940, 1952, 1964, 1976, 1988, 2000	commanding, popular, athletic.
Snake	1941, 1953, 1965, 1977, 1989, 2001	charming, selfish, secretive.
Horse	1942, 1954, 1966, 1978, 1990, 2002	ambitious, popular, fickle.
Goat	1943, 1955, 1967, 1979, 1991, 2003	charming, lucky, unpunctual.
Monkey	1944, 1956, 1968, 1980, 1992, 2004	intelligent, egoistic, entertaining.
Rooster	1945, 1957, 1969, 1981, 1993, 2005	reckless, tactless; imaginative.
Dog	1946, 1958, 1970, 1982, 1994, 2006	watchful, responsible, home-loving.
Pig	1947, 1959, 1971, 1983, 1995, 2007	honest, naïve, kind.

Ultimate
experiences
China
small print

ROUGH GUIDES – don't just travel

We hope you've been inspired by the experiences in this book. To us, they sum up what makes China such an extraordinary and stimulating place to travel. There are 24 other books in the 25 Ultimate Experiences series, each conceived to whet your appetite for travel and for everything the world has to offer. As well as covering the globe, the 25s series also includes books on **Journeys, World Food, Adventure Travel, Places to Stay, Ethical Travel, Wildlife Adventures** and **Wonders of the World**.

When you start planning your trip, Rough Guides' new-look guides, maps and phrasebooks are the ultimate companions. For 25 years we've been refining what makes a good guidebook and we now include more colour photos and more information – on average 50% more pages – than any of our competitors. Just look for the sky-blue spines.

Rough Guides don't just travel – we also believe in getting the most out of life without a passport. Since the publication of the bestselling Rough Guides to **The Internet** and **World Music**, we've brought out a wide range of lively and authoritative guides on everything from **Climate Change** to **Hip-Hop**, from **MySpace** to **Film Noir** and from **The Brain** to **The Rolling Stones**.

Rough Guide credits

Author: David Leffman
Editor: Martin Dunford
Design & picture research: Diana Jarvis
Cartography: Maxine Repath

Cover design: Diana Jarvis
Production: Aimee Hampson, Katherine Owers
Proofreader: Stewart Wild

The author

David Leffman writes Rough Guides to China, Hong Kong, Iceland, Indonesia and Australia.

Picture credits

Publishing information

Rough Guide 25 Ultimate Experiences China Published May 2007 by Rough Guides Ltd, 80 Strand, London WC2R 0RL
345 Hudson St, 4th Floor,
New York, NY 10014, USA
14 Local Shopping Centre, Panchsheel Park, New Delhi 110017, India
Distributed by the Penguin Group
Penguin Books Ltd,
80 Strand, London WC2R 0RL
Penguin Putnam, Inc.
375 Hudson Street, NY 10014, USA
Penguin Group (Australia)
250 Camberwell Road, Camberwell, Victoria 3124, Australia
Penguin Books Canada Ltd,
10 Alcorn Avenue, Toronto, Ontario, Canada M4V 1E4
Penguin Group (NZ)
67 Apollo Drive, Mairangi Bay, Auckland 1310, New Zealand

Printed in China
© Rough Guides 2007

80pp
A catalogue record for this book is available from the British Library
ISBN 1-84353-813-X
ISBN 13: 9781843538134

The publishers and authors have done their best to ensure the accuracy and currency of all the information in **Rough Guide 25 Ultimate Experiences China**, however, they can accept no responsibility for any loss, injury, or inconvenience sustained by any traveller as a result of information or advice contained in the guide.

1   3   5   7   9   8   6   4   2

Fly Less – Stay Longer!

Rough Guides believes in the good that travel does, but we are deeply aware of the impact of fuel emissions on climate change. We recommend taking fewer trips and staying for longer. If you can avoid travelling by air, please use an alternative, especially for journeys of under 1000km/600miles. And always offset your travel at **www.roughguides.com/climatechange**.

ROUGH GUIDES

New Zealand

ROUGH GUIDES

Budapest

ROUGH GUIDES

Thailand

ROUGH GUIDES

Greece

ROUGH GUIDES

Punk

ROUGH GUIDES

Italy

ROUGH GUIDES

India

Over 70 reference books and hundreds of travel
guides, maps & phrasebooks that cover the world.